How to write a scientific paper: The definitive guide to writing and publishing a scientific paper

William V. Jenkins

Index

Introduction

One of the great problems that a person who wants to enter the world of research must face is that he or she has to report the results obtained. This is by no means an easy task, as writing in the scientific world requires the increasingly frequent use of complex words and very specific vocabulary. This guide on how to write and publish a scientific article aims to facilitate a task that for many is the most difficult part of being a researcher.

What are the main motivations for a researcher to publish his or her results?

- First, to build a good academic career. The publications you publish will make you known to a greater or lesser extent.
- If you are looking for a job, the number of published articles and their quality will be decisive.
- You will be able to exchange information and knowledge with other researchers both nationally and internationally.
- No matter how spectacular the results of your experiment or scientific work are, until they are published, they will not be relevant.

Structure of a scientific article

The article is mainly structured in five main differentiated parts (IMRDC): introduction, sample and method, results, discussion, and conclusions. In addition to these, the title, abstract and bibliographical references must also be considered.

The title

What is the title?

The title is the name of a work, the function of which is to designate an object of reality; that is, a title identifies a particular text by functioning as its proper name. In addition to fulfilling an identifying function, it also says something else about its corresponding text, which is why the title is a first bridge to the reader, a communicative act.

This communicative act is also called macrostructure, which synthesises the essential theme or issues of the text. This macrostructure is an abstract representation of the overall structure of the meaning, in this case of the article. Macrostructures are semantic in that they provide a sense of the overall coherence and total meaning of the text. According to the title, the reader will know what the object of the text is and will be able to decide whether he/she finds it interesting.

Academic-scientific titles must be denotative, informative, and autonomous.

Titling is not an easy task. If we get it wrong or are not precise, we can confuse the reader. It should be noted that although the title has a certain level of expressive autonomy, it depends on and is subordinate to the text it represents. For example, there are cases of titles formulated as a question, the answer to which is the article in its entirety.

The title is undoubtedly the most important sentence in the article. The right title often determines whether a reader will pass by your article or whether he or she will read the summary. The title should summaries the main idea of the article. It is a concise statement about the main topic and should identify the actual variables or theoretical aspects under investigation and the relationship between them.

Processing criteria

According to the different manuals and authors, we distinguish, within the criteria for the elaboration of a title, the following sections: lexical selection and wording.

Lexical Selection

The title should include the key words of the subject. Subject words, document descriptors, terms specific to that field of knowledge. Computer systems often use keywords to retrieve documents. Specific terms are preferable to more generic ones. However, you must be careful, as too much specificity can lead to misunderstanding if the reader is unaware of the terms used.
Titles are indexed and compiled in numerous reference works. Therefore, avoid words that do not serve useful purposes, increase length, and may confuse the indexers. For the sake of dissemination, aim for accuracy in the title. No redundancies should appear.

Wording

We read a short title more quickly, we remember it better and we can reproduce it in its entirety as identified in the margin of each page, whereas a long title does not fit on a single line, it must be cut and can also create difficulties in being reproduced. The abusive presence of prepositions is a sign of complexity. We can often eliminate some nouns to avoid the abuse of prepositions. Long titles can be shortened by adding a subtitle underneath. The subtitle will be included in a smaller font.
The title is a statement that clearly and precisely describes the content of an article, in as few words as possible. Avoid abbreviations, symbols and characters that are difficult to

reproduce. When breaking up a title because it does not fit on a single line, the syntagmatic units must be respected.

It is not appropriate to write generic or obvious titles. Nor is it advisable to be cryptic. The title should give clues about the focus of the topic and serve as a common thread. Some prefer to write the headline before the beginning of the text to provide a general framework. Others do it at the end, it is a matter of choice. Due to time constraints, researchers are usually unable to analyse in detail all the immense output in each field or topic in indexing systems, portals, journals, etc. In this sense, an erroneous, imprecise, or very general title can cause us to lose a potential reader who, in the end, is someone who can use our work, criticise it and cite us.

The abstract

A well-crafted abstract is the most important paragraph in the article, and the first piece of information that editors and referees will evaluate. It allows readers to quickly recognise the content and, as with the title, is used in bibliographic index cards, summarisation and retrieval services in libraries and bibliographic and research databases. The abstract strengthens the scientific and linguistic-textual skills of those who write them:

- Scientific since it provides possibilities of access to the article to specialised communities, and at the same time, it is evidence of the appropriation of scientific language.
- Linguistic-textual because multiple skills have to be brought into play in their elaboration. Be clear about the profile of the target audience, the aim of the text, the communicative intention, the context of publication and reading. Recognise the abstract as a genre as well as the article; plan the overall writing, ensure textual coherence, cohesion, and correctness. Use appropriate lexis.

Strategy for drafting the abstract

Abstracting involves the ability and creativity to apply what textual linguistics has called semantic macro-rules, which are very useful for abstract writing, namely: omitting, selecting, generalising, and integrating.

- Omit: this involves removing all information of little importance if it does not have a subsequent function within the text.
- Selecting: this involves choosing the most relevant information for the construction of the abstract.
- Generalising: this consists of replacing a series of concepts with a broader concept that encompasses all of them. In other words, a generic concept.

- Integrate: allows grouping together a series of concepts or ideas that are related to each other or have certain affinity relationships. The aim is to provide new information that derives from and is supported by the data expressed.

Structure and length of the abstract

The research article abstract is a comprehensive summary or objective synthesis of the research that should reflect the structure of the content of the scientific article. It usually has the following rhetorical pattern (IMRC): introduction, methodology, results, and conclusion. This rhetorical pattern is variable depending on the textual typology. This type of summary is called a structured, informative, comprehensive, or analytical summary.

- Introduction: statement of the problem, objectives and scope of the research.
- Methodology: information on the methodological design. How the study was carried out.
- Results: most relevant findings.
- Conclusion: the main summary of the study is presented.

It should be noted that the abstract does not attempt to give an exhaustive account of all the above, but rather to select and present the most essential parts of each section in order to give the reader a basic idea of the research work. The ideal abstract consists of four parts answering four questions:

- Part 1: What is the problem/the subject of this article?
- Part 2: How is it solved (methodology)?
- Part 3: What results have been obtained and to what extent is the problem solved?
- Part 4: So what? To what extent is this article useful for science/the reader?

In analytical or structured abstracts, it is advisable to dedicate an average of two to three lines to each section, depending on the length indicated by the journal in its publication criteria. In academic communities and journals, there is the idea that anyone who does not follow these conventions is evidence of a lack of scientific rigour.

Recommendations for the drafting of abstracts

1. Before writing the abstract, you should bear in mind that this is the first part of the article that the editors and reviewers will read in order to decide whether to accept it or not.

2. Do not waste space by repeating the title of the article.

3. Abstracts should reflect the structure of the article they accompany.
4. Avoid criticism and interpretation, as abstracts are essentially informative and expository, and should function as self-contained texts, as they are generally disseminated independently.

5. The abstract should be self-sufficient and intelligible to the reader.

6. Avoid including isolated quotations or references, abbreviations, symbols, graphic formulae, characters in other alphabets, examples, and negative statements in the abstract.

7. The abstract should not present any information or conclusions that are not in the article.

8. Do not write the abstract in the first person.

9. Do not include unnecessary details in the abstract (you need to know what information to omit).

Finally, the abstract should, firstly, state the main objectives and scope of the research; secondly, describe the methods used; thirdly, present the results; and fourthly, state the most important conclusions.

The keywords

Keywords are the most relevant terms that are developed in the text. According to the indications of each journal, generally 3 to 5 keywords are presented in strict alphabetical order. Keywords serve several functions:

- They allow the reader/researcher to verify that the article may be on the topic of interest.
- They help to locate the correct article quickly and efficiently in scientific databases, libraries...
- They make it possible to abstract and bring together articles on the same topic (review).
- They allow editors to identify reviewers in relation to the topics of the article.
- They constitute a controlled language (discipline-specific terminology).

Keywords are not necessarily isolated lexical units but can be compound words or nominal groups (a set of words that have a noun or noun at their core). For example, if you want to present "the higher education forum" as a keyword, this nominal group, consisting of five lexical units, constitutes a "keyword".

All keywords must be included exactly between the title and the abstract.

The introduction

The introduction is the letter of introduction to the rest of the article, through which the reader gets a precise idea of the content of the article.

Among the aspects that a good introduction should include and develop are the following:

- Theoretical framework of the work. Here the principles or theories that underpin the research are cited and briefly described.
- Statement of the problem. A brief description of the research problem to be solved with the work in question.
- The background of the work. Previous studies by other authors on the same topic addressed in the article are analysed.
- In the case of a review of works related to ours, it is advisable to go deeper and to critically analyse them. Thus, for example, the similarities and differences between previous works and ours should be noted, as well as the limitations of previous works that we intend to remedy now, etc.
- Objectives of the work. These should be clearly and simply formulated and, obviously, should correspond to the results and conclusions obtained.

Importance of the introduction

They highlight the importance and centrality of the topic. They provide an overview of the main previous research by means of expanding references. They formulate the objectives of the text. Finally, they explain the structure of the document.

Extension of the introduction

Placing the research in the context of previous relevant work. Relevant previous work written by others. Explain the reasons for carrying out the study. Mention the methods used. Note the conclusions to be drawn from the results.

It should occupy about 10-15% of the total article, approx.

The methodology

Without a strong Methods section, writers will not be able to convince readers of the validity of the means used to obtain the findings.

Methodology is a demonstrative element that strengthens the credibility of the findings to be reported later. Methods and techniques used in previous research are often cited in the methods section to attract the interest of professional readers and to suggest that the methods used are the most appropriate for the research design.

This section provides specific information on the methodological design of the research, how the study was (or is being) conducted, the procedures or methods used, the tools, the participants, and the scope of the work. The discursive organisation of this methodology section is essentially descriptive-expositive, sometimes with a chronological criterion or according to the logical stages of the research design. It is presented in detail:
- The tools.
- The materials.
- The samples.
- The corpus.
- The participants.
- The scope of the work.
- The procedures that were required to arrive at the research results.

Methods should reflect the order in which the results were obtained. Thus, ideally, the section should:
- Identify the source of the data and the method used to collect it.
- Describe the experimental procedures and the methods adopted to process the data.
- Describe the procedures adopted in the analysis of

the data (including statistical tests).

Sources

In biology, medicine, etc., if human or animal testing has been performed, the section begins with an explanation of the protocol followed in the institution (or international standards/conventions).

Some general "guidelines", which are common in qualitative research. Methodological approach, type of study/scope: what kind of research is it? General procedure for developing the study: descriptive, analytical, applied.

Design

This explains how the research is designed. Conceptual categories (what concepts guide your work and will guide your analysis?) Formation of the corpus or the object of study/sample for the sample for the analysis (how is the corpus formed?). Criteria (what were the criteria for choosing the corpus?). Description of the samples for analysis (the corpus is described). Data collection techniques (data collection techniques are stated, e.g., literature review in scientific databases such as...). Systematisation (how was the information collected organised/coded? In some cases, a preliminary data analysis can be carried out).

Some disciplines have other (sometimes explicit) subsections in the Methods section.

The results

Before you start writing the results section, pause for a moment to remember your purpose. In this section you are going to take the reader on a path that follows the steps of your reasoning, as well as the sequence of your experiments from your working hypothesis (or the definition of the purpose of your study) to a conclusion that corresponds exactly to the title of your article.

This section summarises the most relevant data collected, and the type of analysis carried out. It is one of the sections that contributes most to knowledge. Data should be presented in sufficient detail to justify the conclusions.

Questions to focus the results writing process.

1. What do my results say? (brief summary of the main points)

2. What do these results mean in context? (conclusions that can be drawn)
3. What do you need to know about these results (what does the audience need to know about the results you are writing about)?

4. What do they need to know for? (what will they miss if they don't read it?)

Data quality

Only experimental results that are absolutely reproducible should be published. You should ensure that your results are reproducible by performing each experiment several times, if possible. Your article serves not only to communicate your findings to others, but also to allow others to repeat your experiments and build new science from them. Therefore, if you cannot obtain reproducible results, it is unlikely that anyone else will be able to do so, and therefore your results are not worthy of publication. The validity of the results also depends on the size of the sample: the larger the sample, the higher the value of its results.

Results vs. Discussion

Some journals allow and even suggest the condensation of Results and Discussion into a single section entitled "Results and Discussion".

Many authors present results and discussion in a single section, when the topic under study gives rise to several results that by their nature need to be analysed as they are presented. In this case, you can discuss the significance of each result after presenting the relevant data and end the whole article with a few concluding sentences summarising the study, its importance, and the possible or actual direction for future research. Also, when the discussion is relatively brief and straightforward, some authors prefer to combine it with the "results" section, which produces "Results and Discussion" or "Results and Conclusions".

Graphical aids: tables, graphs and their relationship to the text

Figures include photographs, drawings, graphs and diagrams. Tables are all those tables prepared in Word or Excel (grouped data, figures, chronologies, statistics).

What are they useful for?

These resources serve to show in a clearer and simpler way ideas and facts that the written text could not present with equal efficiency. Proper design, selection and presentation of this material is essential for articles to achieve their expository objectives. Tables, graphs, drawings, etc. are often very useful (sometimes even necessary) for the presentation of results. But there are some guidelines to bear in mind between these graphics and writing:

- Try not to repeat tediously in the text what is already evident from a careful reading of the tables. The text should emphasise important observations and present them in decreasing order of interest, starting with the main finding. Tables are used to report the details of the result.
- Tables for number, individual data and precise data.
- Graphs and figures for shapes, general data and approximate data.

The choice of whether to use a graph, table or text display depends on the content or meaning we want the reader to receive from the data. Each form of data visualisation has strengths and weaknesses.

Tables are most useful if they are searched:
- Recording data (raw or processed data).
- Explaining calculations or showing components of the calculated data.
- Show the actual values of the data and their accuracy.
- Allowing multiple comparisons between items in many directions.

Graphics are most useful for:
- Show a general trend or image.
- Understanding the story through "form" rather than actual numbers.
- Allowing simple comparisons between only a few elements.

How to number the graphic material?

Each table and figure will start with independent numbering. For example, if an article includes two tables and two figures, these must appear with their respective title and independent numbering.

Common defects in graphics:
- The wrong type of chart has been chosen and the relationships between elements are either a) not obvious when they are important or b) explicit when they do not exist.
- Weak descriptive titles are used when a narrative title would be appropriate.
- Data shown in the text or tables are repeated in the graph.
- The shape, shading, pattern or thickness of symbols, markers or lines does not emphasise the main results.
- The graph is unnecessarily cluttered with lines, legend, symbols, numbers, etc., and axis scale divisions are poorly chosen.
- Axes are not labelled descriptively.
- Numbers are included when exact values are not important for the story and approximate values can be derived from the X and Y axes.

Tables:

Tables are often used to record the data of a study and may contain a number of rows or columns that require careful reading by the user to appreciate their meaning. This is especially true when tables contain a large number of cells and when comparisons between different rows and columns are necessary to understand the results. These potential limitations of tables can largely be overcome with good design, particularly in terms of the layout of the table, the choice of data for inclusion, order of data within the table, and the presence of an effective table title and row/column headings. Many of the visual design elements are common to those discussed for graphics: keeping tables uncluttered and defining abbreviations in the table title or using footnotes.

The discussion

If it is decided to separate "results" from "discussion".

Once the results have been presented, you proceed to evaluate and interpret their implications, especially as they relate to the main purpose of the research. The data can be freely examined, interpreted and qualified and inferences can be drawn from them. It is recommended to emphasise the theoretical implications of the results, the significance of the results and the validity of the conclusions.

Some aspects of organising a good discussion section:
- Present the principles, relationships and scope of the results.
- State exceptions, lack of correlation, and existence of uncertainties.
- Interpret the results in comparison with published work.
- Clearly discuss the implications of the work.
- Take care that each aspect discussed is demonstrated by the results of the work.

Many articles, which may be attractive because of their subject matter, literature review, scientific methodology, and interesting and valid results, are rejected or have little impact because of poor discussion. Many discussions are long and lush, dubious and obscure, getting lost in a sea of words.

The Discussion section should summarise the results and indicate whether the hypothesis has been corroborated or refuted. If the results can be explained by any rival hypothesis, it is a sign of intellectual integrity to make that possibility explicit here, along with the reasons why you believe that alternative explanations are either legitimate or not viable.
- Rival hypotheses are those that are presented as an

answer to a problem and have successfully passed empirical tests.

- Auxiliary Hypotheses are those that are used as a complement for testing. This testing depends on the veracity of the Auxiliary Hypotheses for its result.
- Ad Hoc Hypothesis is a hypothesis that is introduced for the sole purpose of saving a hypothesis seriously threatened by adverse testimony.

Advice:

1. The results should be evaluated, not the author.

2. Try not to claim that "I am the first": someone you don't know can always come along who has worked on something similar.

3. The Discussion should also include interesting lines that remain open for future research.

4. Start as many sentences as possible with the subject. Try to ensure that there are no more than ten words before the subject and that there are only a few occasions when there are. Check introductory subordinate clauses and turn them into independent sentences where possible.

5. Insecure writers tend to start too many sentences with I think, I believe or in my opinion. Readers already assume that you believe and think what you write: don't say it.

The conclusions

Some authors separate the discussion from the conclusions. In this case, they limit each as follows:
- Discussion: commentary on the results.
- Conclusion: analysis and general summary of the whole article.

It can be said that conclusions, in the case of academic and research articles, do not constitute a synthesis or a summary or a summary paraphrased with elements from the introduction of the paper or article.

The conclusions, a section in which the results and implications of the research or the proposed reflection are presented and interpreted, tend to be formulated with a dialogical intention (interaction with the reader).

The conclusions are a mandatory section with rhetorical purposes typical of academic and research texts, whether they are partial advances or definitive results.

In the case of research advances or results, conclusions do not imply that the work or project has been concluded, but rather that this particular text presents, in accordance with its scope and objectives, conclusions structured according to different discursive movements, which may be:
- Strengths and weaknesses of the research (a critical view of the results is presented).
- Evaluation and implications of the results or findings of the work (analysis of the contributions of the work compared to previous, similar work or within the framework of a given problem).
- In writing the conclusions, the hypotheses should be kept in mind, which should be analysed in accordance with the data obtained in the analysis (hypothesising the explanation of the results).

- Open questions and probable further lines of research in the framework of the results obtained.
- Possible applications, recommendations or suggestions are projected.

Useful recommendations for drafting conclusions

1. Conclusions should be derived from the results and discussion in the previous sections.

2. It is not advisable for the conclusions to be a repetition of the summary that heads every article.

3. The discussion of results should not be confused with the drawing of conclusions, which depend as much on the results and their analysis as on the theoretical framework and objectives.

4. This section, in addition to the conclusions as such, makes explicit recommendations for further research, such as suggesting new questions, and indicates what follows and should be done.

5. The implications of the research are assessed.

6. How the research questions were answered and whether or not the objectives were met.

7. The results are related to other studies.

8. Discuss limitations of the research.

9. Unexpected results are explained.

10. When hypotheses are not tested, it is necessary to point out or analyse the reasons.

11. Conclusions are not a repetition of results, but a summary of the most important results.

12. Conclusions should be consistent with the data.

Bibliographical references

The list of references at the end of a scientific journal article documents it and provides the information necessary to identify and locate each source. Authors should choose references wisely and include only those sources that were used in the research and preparation of the article.

References cited in the article should be included in the final list of references. In the review process, the author should check that each source cited appears in both places. The in-text citation and the entry in the reference list must be identical in their spelling and year.

As for the style of the bibliographic reference, each journal proposes its own format.

Normally, in internal quotations in the text, if the quotation is longer than three lines, it usually appears as a full stop with an indentation and a smaller font number. If the quotation is shorter, it will follow the last sentence and be enclosed in inverted commas. In any case, it is necessary to refer to the internal regulations of each magazine.

Writing a text

Ask yourself whether your ideas are interesting to you and why they would be interesting to other people. New ideas are difficult to accept. The more your ideas deviate from the mainstream, the more effort you have to put into your article to convince people that what you have to say is worth listening to.

Be truthful, clear, well organised and direct. Write linearly. Avoid jargon where possible, but if you need to, be sure to define unfamiliar terms. Make it clear what is new in your article. Often, it is not so clear to the reader. Make sure you make it explicit, rather than relying on readers to see it. Think about the people who are likely to review your article and the kinds of objections they may raise. Referees represent many other readers, who may see things differently from you and who need to be convinced of the validity of what you say.

Write in the form of an hourglass. Start your article with the general questions you will address. Then be more specific in telling what you have done. Finally, discuss at length the implications of your work. Make it clear how your study tests your hypothesis. Polish and correct. Don't expect referees or editors to rewrite it for you, and don't expect them to tolerate sloppy, sloppy or error-laden writing. Poor writing is enough of an argument to reject an entire article, even if the research it contains is good.

Don't use synonyms, especially for technical terms, just because you want to avoid redundancy. Readers may think you are varying the words you use because you are referring to different concepts. Adapt the length of the article proportionally to your contribution: the longer you make your article, the bigger your contribution needs to be otherwise, shorten it.

Use a title that clearly expresses what the article is about and, if possible, is also attention-grabbing. Write an abstract that contains the information that a reader would be most interested in knowing. Keep in mind that many people will never read beyond your abstract. The better your abstract captures the key ideas and conclusions of your article, the better your work will be disseminated (they may cite you without reading it). Accept feedback non-defensively, but critically: most of the comments you receive from referees will help you produce a better article, but some will not.

A good author writes with his or her readers in mind. Ask yourself to what extent they will be able to understand what you write. A good article has a message to remember: Often readers finish an article without having a clear idea of what the main point of the article is supposed to be. Write for a group or type of magazines: You should have a magazine or class of magazines in mind when writing an article. This way, the article can be targeted to the readers and can meet the requirements of that magazine or group of magazines.

Choose carefully the journal to which you submit your article. You can save yourself a lot of time by choosing a journal that is appropriate for what it publishes. Don't take reviews personally: the comments are about the work, not about you. When you resubmit the article after revising it, be clear that you have to handle each and every point raised in the comments: Reviewers and editors get annoyed when they are ignored. You should follow most of their suggestions and indicate how you have done so in a resubmission letter. Those suggestions that you will not accept should be highlighted in the letter, along with an explanation of why you have not followed them.
Use direct quotations only when necessary, such as to convey the exact message of an original text. Otherwise, they only get in the way and often obscure your message. State

your research question clearly: You need to be very clear about what issues will be addressed in your article. Handle differences of opinion with respect. Treat others as you would want them to treat you, even if you disagree with what they say. Be generous in your quotations from other authors. No one likes to be ignored, especially article referees. It is important to cite relevant previous work as well, especially if any of that work is by a potential referee of your article. It is also important to cite papers that are not in line with your point of view, as well as those that are.

Try to keep up to date with the literature in your field: no one likes to read an article whose author has obviously stopped keeping up with the latest developments in the field a decade ago. This does not exclude older but quality works. Ask your colleagues (or editor) to read your paper and comment on it before submitting it to a journal. Mention what the structure of each part is going to be: it is often difficult for readers to follow the story line in an article. By providing the top-down structure and making it transparent how the article will be organised, you make it easier for readers to understand what you have to say.

Choose the order of the results that best conveys the message you want to convey. Find a common thread. Justify your choice of statistical tests. Don't assume that readers will know why you did the tests you did. Explain why you did them. Make sure your conclusions follow from your data: It is often tempting for an author to go beyond the data in drawing conclusions, saying what he or she wants to conclude rather than what the data allow him or her to conclude. Decide what is worth emphasising in your discussion and what is not: Good writing is hierarchical: Make it clear which points are important and which are merely supporting points.

Publication process

Why is it difficult to publish in a journal?

Difficulties related to writing. Problems in expressing ideas in a clear and orderly manner; problems with the conventions of the journal; problems with the vehicular language.

Difficulties related to the topic. Not all research is novel (or new) or of sufficient scientific interest. Scientific journals have special requirements that can be difficult to meet: publishing, including scientific publishing, is a business.

Author-related (psychological) difficulties. Communicating our work to the world makes us a potential target for criticism. The process of advancing knowledge is confrontational; new ideas and results are hotly debated. Thus, authors who are faced with the blank page and thus a potentially critical recipient may find writing a daunting process.

Solution

To think that by submitting an article to an international journal, we are actually becoming part of a big international conversation. To do this, we need to know what has been said before and what is being said right now in the important circles of the discipline worldwide. We must have access to journals where colleagues publish; subscribe to journal alerts; and be trained in database and web searching.

The editorial process

Before you start writing your article, you should also consider how many people are likely to find your work interesting. If you are working in a very small field, it is likely that your colleagues and competitors will all publish in the same journals and that these journals will have a relatively small circulation.

Criteria for the choice of the scientific journal

Choose the magazine before writing the article or after? Ideally before. Problems: rejections, differences between disciplines.

Particularise or generalist journals? The larger the readership of a given journal, the more difficult it is to publish in that journal. For example, the editors of Science accept only 10 per cent of papers submitted for review and reject approximately 65 per cent of manuscripts submitted to Science within a week to ten days of receipt.

Balance: the more general, the more rejection. The more particular, the less impact. However, in the first instance you should aim high and try to publish your article in the best possible journal in your field.

Many journals now require electronic submission of manuscripts and the instructions for submission can be quite complicated, particularly when figures and tables are part of the manuscript. Before making a final decision on which journal to choose, carefully examine the most recent issues and check that your research is appropriate for the journal. Then study the Instructions to Authors carefully to make sure you can submit your manuscript in the required format. Studying the Instructions to Authors may lead to a shocking discovery: some journal editors make you pay for the privilege of having your manuscript published in one of their journals.

The readership of a journal is largely determined by the scope and objectives of the journal, the journal's reputation and publishing history in the field, as well as the accessibility of the journal to researchers (e.g., is it expensive, does it have an open access option for authors, is it published by a small publisher with limited distribution).

Electronic journals

Internet access to journal titles, abstracts and web pages has made many more journals accessible to a wider audience. However, some users do not wish to pay for access to a document, so free journals will, for practical purposes, have a wider audience. New journals may also take time to build an audience. Visit the journal and publisher's website to see if the journal you are considering is widely distributed.

Impact factor

There is no simple way to assess the quality of a journal or the contribution of a journal to a scientific discipline over time. For this reason, indices have been developed that provide information on the speed and citation volume of journals, so that these indices can give some guidance on the popularity and use of journals. The most commonly used measure of journal impact is the impact factor. The Impact Factor for a given year is the average number of times articles published in the journal in the previous two years have been cited in that year: This index provides an average of the recent use of articles in a given journal.

Use of journal quality indexes
The indexes described above primarily measure the citation rate or citation volume of the average article in a journal: they are measures of the journal and not of individual articles. The number of citations of your article can also be calculated and can be higher or lower than the journal average. The indexes are calculated from a selected list of journals; this list largely excludes journals published in non-

English speaking countries and does not usually include new journals that are still gaining a reputation.

Time of publication

Journals want to publish incoming articles quickly, to make sure they attract authors who are doing new and innovative work. You may need to publish your research quickly to make sure that no one else publishes similar work before you, or you may want to increase your publication and citation record for promotions and grants. If publication time is important to you, check the magazine's website or recent issues to see if they report the average time to publication. Magazines that publish an online version of the newspaper before the print version generally take less time to publish.

Authors' relationship with journals

Sending my proposal

Five practices to optimise publication results:
- Reviewing manuscripts for colleagues and journals; thus, developing a solid framework for both scientific writing and critiquing the work of others.
- Plan your research and writing to meet the quality assurance criteria that referees, and editors will impose on you.
- Carefully select the journal to be submitted to and prepare the manuscript content and style to maximise the chances of acceptance.
- Use structured and thorough peer review and pre-review processes to improve the manuscript before submission.
- Use referees' reports to improve the manuscript and clearly show the journal editor that the requested improvements have been made.

Understanding the peer review process

The peer review process helps the scientific community to ensure the quality of research before it is published and before it can be examined and used by a wider public. Peer review is part of the process of turning information into knowledge. The correspondence between author, reviewer and editor is part of a collective sense-making process used to prove that new information is worth knowing and acting upon.

The peer review confirms that the hypotheses have been adequately tested and that the reported results are supported by the materials, methods and analytical tools used. It also confirms that the strength of the claims about the results and implications of the study are appropriate. Assists journals in deciding whether the focus, novelty, and significance of the research are appropriate for the level of the journal. Checks that the presentation and style of content conforms to accepted conventions. Advises authors and the journal editor on how (and often where) the manuscript could be improved.

Reviewers are important to the journal editor because they play a critical role in determining the quality of manuscripts, and in most cases do so as a professional and unpaid contribution. Referees are important to the author because they bring a critical eye to the content and writing and highlight how the story can be clarified or better presented. Responding to a reviewer's comments should be seen as part of the process of testing and legitimising your research results and their significance.

Understanding the role of the editor

The editor is responsible for maintaining the reputation and competitiveness of the journal. Editors use referees to assist them in screening manuscripts and improving them for publication. The editor will read the manuscript and make the initial decision on whether it will be sent to reviewers. The editor will usually reject a manuscript without review only if:
- The manuscript is outside the scope or objectives of the journal.
- The language or structure of the manuscript is deficient.
- There are clear or obvious flaws in the research.

Author's cover letter

The cover letter you send to the editor with your manuscript (or upload in the appropriate box on the journal's website) is an important opportunity to sell your article. The letter is an opportunity to show that you appreciate the editor's role and that you have done your best to prepare the manuscript to meet the journal's requirements (thus making the editor's job easier). Express your conviction that the article is within the scope of the journal. State the title of the manuscript and the names of the authors. State that the research and the article are new and original. Highlight specific points that reinforce the novelty and importance of the research. Say that you are waiting for the reviewers' comments.

Reviewers

This work is generally unpaid and is carried out as part of the researchers' professional contribution to the development of their scientific field. Reviewers:
-   They are usually experts in the general field of the article (not necessarily experts in the exact topic of the article they are reviewing).
-   They have almost always published work in the general field (possibly work that you have cited in your article).
-   They are busy with their own research, writing, teaching, administration, etc.
-   They are willing to review manuscripts but have limited time and patience.
-   They have their own preferences and prejudices about scientific research and the way it is written.

You will not know who the reviewers are, but in many cases, depending on the journal's policy, the reviewers will know the names of the authors. Reviewers will be asked to read the manuscript and write a report on the quality of the paper, note any problems and recommend changes that would improve the manuscript: The reviewer is usually asked to complete a manuscript quality assessment form, and may also be asked to recommend whether the manuscript should be accepted by the journal or accepted after revisions.

The reviewer will return their written report and evaluation form to the editor, sometimes with annotations on the manuscript itself (although this is now less common with electronic submission).

Acceptance of the paper

When the research is interesting and new, but the manuscript requires significant work before it is acceptable, the editor may reject the article, but encourages the author to rewrite and resubmit it. A specific date is usually given for the new shipment with the modifications.